My First Acrostic

Southern Counties

Edited by Donna Samworth

First published in Great Britain in 2009 by:

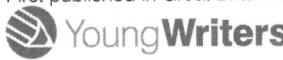

Young Writers
Remus House
Coltsfoot Drive
Peterborough
PE2 9JX
Telephone: 01733 890066
Website: www.youngwriters.co.uk

All Rights Reserved
© Copyright Contributors 2009
SB ISBN 978-1-84924-627-9

Foreword

The 'My First Acrostic' collection was developed by Young Writers specifically for Key Stage 1 children. The poetic form is simple, fun and gives the young poet a guideline to shape their ideas, yet at the same time leaves room for their imagination and creativity to begin to blossom.

Due to the young age of the entrants we have enjoyed rewarding their effort by including as many of the poems as possible. Our hope is that seeing their work in print will encourage the children to continue writing as they grow and develop their skills into our poets of tomorrow.

Young Writers was established in 1990 to nurture creativity in our children and young adults, to give them an interest in poetry and an outlet to express themselves. This latest collection will act as a milestone for the young poets and one that will be enjoyable to revisit again and again.

Contents

Andover CE Primary School, Andover
Olivia Payne (6) 1
Jasmine Munro (6) 2
James Munnery-Tyler (6) 3
James Potter (5) 4
Chloe Eaton (6) 5
Skye Ware (6) 6
Euan Tims (6) 7
Meadow Dallimore (6) 8
Charlotte Lattimer (7) 9
Shaina Baines (7) 10
Hugh Tims (7) 11
Luke Stone (7) 12
Mhairi Sergent (7) 13
Harry Moule (7) 14
Emily Eaton (7) 15
Kira Dunn (7) 16

Bitterne Manor Primary School, Southampton
Elizabeth Hickman (7) 17
Elizabeth Brading (6) 18
Aleeza Mabood (7) 19
Heather Brennan (6) 20
Darren Sutherland (7) 21
Thomas Dawson (7) 22
Beth Berman-Hughes (7) 23
Rueben Whitehead (7) 24
Abigail Page (7) 25
Jasmine Sainsbury (7) 26
Riley Whitehead (7) 27
Gian Chahal (7) 28
Brooke Lewis (7) 29

Chalgrove School, Chalgrove
Isobel Taylor (7) 30
Holly Crosthwaite (6) 31
Connor Caffel (7) 32
Tom Mercer (6) 33
Ciara Rogers (7) 34
Kera Baker (7) 35
Beatrice Justice (6) 36

Olivia Soper (6) 37
Thomas Marriage (7) 38
Thomas Harrison (6) 39
William Fern (7) 40
Charlotte Arnold (6) 41
Kyle Watts (7) 42
Mia Richardson (7) 43
Charlie Smith (7) 44
Kieran Law (6) 45
Naomi Forsyth (7) 46
Jack Carter (6) 47
Charlotte Grehan (7) 48
Harrison Todd (6) 49
Mia Moores (6) 50

Combe CE Primary School, Witney
Conrad Peck (6) 51
Josh Stares (7) 52
Axel Stares (6) 53
Joseph Creasey (6) 54
Aidan Paterson (6) 55
George Bugler (7) 56
Bethany Paine (6) 57
Olivia Westbrook (7) 58
Hannah Sheppard (6) 59
Matilda Bugler (6) 60
Connor Kirby (7) 61
Isobel Shone (7) 62
Georgia Nicholson (6) 63
Isla Henderson (6) 64
Ella Evans (7) 65
Millie Blakesley-Grimes (7) 66

Forest & Sandridge CE Primary School, Melksham
Thomas Greatwood (7) 67
Joseph White (7) 68
Casey Herron (7) 69
Freya Wyatt (7) 70
Owen Wood (7) 71
Tye Sullivan (7) 72
Brandon Humphries (7) 73
Brendan Harvey (7) 74

Eloise Hatfield (7) 75
Michael Wilkins (7) 76
Amy Vines (7) 77
Isobel Godsell (7) 78
Chloe Bowden (7) 79
Paige Charman (7) 80
Evie Fish (6) 81
Max Bramley (7) 82
Milly Bannister (6) 83
Scott Atkins (7) 84
Richard Andrews (7) 85

Harestock Primary School, Winchester

Lucas Soedring (7) 86
Adam Fisher 87
Mieszko Stabolepszy (7) 88
Oliver Hayes 89
Laura Soper (7) 90
Michael George (7) 91
Matthew Hoyland (7) 92
Maisie Stead 93
Ryan Barker (7) 94
Abbie Hamilton (7) 95
Amber Mears 96
Lily Smithers (7) 97
Kitty Chappell (6) 98

Highnam Primary School, Highnam

Charlotte McDowall (7) 99

Longleaze Primary School, Swindon

Swathan Meenakumar (7) 100
Max Hopkins (6) 101
Megan Lockett
& Charlie Lambert (6) 102
Pheobe Doe (6) 103
Thea Hopkins (6) 104

Medina Primary School, Cosham

Billy Smith (6) 105
Daisy-May English (5) 106
Jayden Ridout (6) 107
Hannah Goodwin (6) 108
Kai Passingham-Hutchings (5) 109
Jack Goodwin (6) 110

Ryan Armstrong (6) 111
Cain Wallace (6) 112
Nivara Gregory (6) 113
Tulula Romer (6) 114
Keeley Newell (6) 115
Archie Drury (6) 116
Jimmy Cook (6) 117
Shannon-Marie Harvell (6) 118
Daniela Monen (6) 119

Meysey Hampton CE Primary School, Cirencester

Finlay Hawkins (7) 120
Miles Farrington (7) 121
Ashley Stutzman (7) 122
Joscelyn Moore (6) 123
Patrick Wright (6) 124
Natasha Gleeson (6) 125
Joshua Mason (6) 126
Poppy Nicholls (7) 127
Molly Davies (6) 128
Alex Finnegan (6) 129
Jamie Whitehouse (6) 130

Millbrook Primary School, Wantage

Katie Jarvey (6) 131
Sam Cheshire (6) 132
Amy Simcock (6) 133
Dylan Drake (6) 134
Sophie Jones (6) 135
Emily McArdle (6) 136
Michael Hollier (6) 137

Newton Tony CE Primary School, Salisbury

Clara Henley (6) 138
Luke Houghton (7) 139

St George's Beneficial School, Portsmouth

Madina Islam 140
Laura Coombes (7) 141
Owen Scrivens (7) 142
Felicity Walker 143
Owen Whiteaway (7) 144
Stan Griffin 145
Rakan Alromayon (7) 146
Logan Clark 147

Chloe Cheshire (6) 148
Semilore Fagbola (7) 149

St Jude's RC Primary School, Fareham

Benjamin Lolljowaheer (6) 150
Francesca Fryers (7) 151
Reuben Menezes (6) 152
Moyo Odude (7) 153
Thomas Wylde (7) 154
Thomas Bruce (7) 155
Byron Snook (7) 156
Holly Cristofoli (7) 157
Daniel Chadwick (6) 158
Andrew Evans (7) 159
Ryan Hockaday (7) 160
Finlay Harrison (7) 161
Emma Bolwell (6) 162
Emma Wright (7) 163
Lucas Miles (6) 164
Fred Hamilton (7) 165
Ciaran Miskella (7) 166
Finn Judge (7) 167
Libby Choularton (7) 168
Owen Joice (7) 169
Sophie-Jade Humphrey (7) 170
Sarah Collins (6) 171

Standlake CE Primary School, Standlake

Hope Swain (7) 172
Joshua Gauntlett (6) 173
Will Ellett (6) 174
Jacob Denmark Fyfe (6) 175
Grace Soame (7) 176
Josh Barber (6) 177
Jonah King (6) 178
William Woodford (7) 179
Jamie Beland (7) 180
Becky Evans (6) 181
Morganna Swain (7) 182
Savannah Willans (6) 183

Stratford-Sub-Castle School, Salisbury

Daniel Hobbs (6) 184
Scarlett Cooper 185

Gabrielle Ashton (7) 186
Ashley Nuccio (7) 187
Samuel Webb (7) 188
Russell Read (6) 189
Sadie Montgomery (7) 190
Aliesha Hirang (6) 191
Scott Gray (7) 192
Harvey Guilder (6) 193
Harry Lewis (6) 194
Fern Crumbie (5) 195

The Grey House School, Hartley Wintney

Jack Coldrick (5) 196
Clemmie Quilter-Wood (5) 197
William Barnfield (5) 198
Sophie Pearce-Molland (6) 199
Isobel Young (6) 200
Charlie Warren (6) 201
Louis Sykes (5) 202
Alfie Smallwood (6) 203
Finlay Anderson (6) 204
Luca Tonkin (6) 205
Amelia Trist (6) 206
Frida Kenning (5) 207

The Poems

My First Acrostic - Southern Counties

Olivia

O livia can play with her dog.
L oves lots of ice lollies all the time.
I eat ice cream.
V ery yummy it is too.
I can play with my sister
A nd Amy.

Olivia Payne (6)
Andover CE Primary School, Andover

Jasmine

J asmine has a big bear.
A cat comes in the garden.
S ad when cats die.
M ummy is good at cooking food.
I n the morning I have breakfast.
N ever being naughty.
E very day I give my mummy a kiss.

Jasmine Munro (6)
Andover CE Primary School, Andover

My First Acrostic - Southern Counties

James

J ames likes jelly
A nd football
M ason is my friend
E ats biscuits
S ings happy songs.

James Munnery-Tyler (6)
Andover CE Primary School, Andover

James

J ames likes football
A nd likes kick-boxing too
M ainly is good in class
E very day does his best
S ometimes is silly

P lays really nicely.

James Potter (5)
Andover CE Primary School, Andover

My First Acrostic - Southern Counties

Chloe

C hloe likes to play.

H er mum gives her breakfast.

L ikes to sleep.

O n my dad's Father's Day I give my dad a card.

E mily and me play with my friends.

Chloe Eaton (6)
Andover CE Primary School, Andover

Skye

S kye likes to play on the computer.
K ind and gentle.
Y es can be helpful.
E njoys school.

Skye Ware (6)
Andover CE Primary School, Andover

My First Acrostic - Southern Counties

Euan

E uan likes to eat.
U sually I have strawberry ice cream.
A ll the time I play Lego and football.
N obody thinks I'm silly.

Euan Tims (6)
Andover CE Primary School, Andover

Meadow

M eadow is a monkey
E very day she swings from tree to tree
A nd she likes to eat bananas all day
D on't get the bananas
O r she'll eat you
W hy are people chopping down the trees?

Meadow Dallimore (6)
Andover CE Primary School, Andover

Charlotte

C harlotte is very kind and helpful.
H as a cat that is restless in the night.
A very good helper.
R eally likes tap-dancing.
L oves cold drinks.
O ak trees are her favourite tree.
T ap-dancing is very fun indeed.
T aking care of her sister.
E ats Lincolnshire sausages.

Charlotte Lattimer (7)
Andover CE Primary School, Andover

Shaina

S uper, super good like gold
H as a hamster that smells like food
A nd likes to pick cherries with a glove
I ce is very yummy when it's cold like ice cream
N ever gives up no matter what
A nd never perfect in whatever she does.

Shaina Baines (7)
Andover CE Primary School, Andover

My First Acrostic - Southern Counties

Hugh

H eroic Hugh!
U nsteady Hugh is always steady,
G oes shopping all the time.
H ugh is a very good footballer!

T iger teaser
I hate writing!
M y best friend is Kira!
S impsons fan!

Hugh Tims (7)
Andover CE Primary School, Andover

Luke

L oves teddies
U ses teddies in bed
K ing of the world
E xcellent boy.

Luke Stone (7)
Andover CE Primary School, Andover

Mhairi

M olly is magnificent.

H ugh is hilarious.

A bigale loves the alphabet.

I sabelle is intelligent.

R alph is rude.

I sabelle isn't really intelligent.

Mhairi Sergent (7)
Andover CE Primary School, Andover

Harry Moule

H appy Harry all day long.
A mazing Harry jumps all day long.
R unning happily in the wind.
R uns like mad.
Y ou are the fastest.

M oule is my surname.
O ld Harry is fabulous at football.
U tterly fabulous at golf.
L ove to go to the park.
E ven sometimes happy.

Harry Moule (7)
Andover CE Primary School, Andover

My First Acrostic - Southern Counties

Emily

E xactly no one like me looks like me.
M y hamster is annoying when it is running on its wheel.
I ncredible at ice skating!
L oves ice cream in any sort of way!
Y ummy ice cubes cool me down on hot, summery days.

Emily Eaton (7)
Andover CE Primary School, Andover

Kira

K ind Kira is queen of the world.
I nteresting Kira is all the time.
R unning Kira goes through the door.
A mazing Kira all the time.

Kira Dunn (7)
Andover CE Primary School, Andover

My First Acrostic - Southern Counties

On Safari

O n Planet Earth in Africa
N ot in England

S itting on the ground
A t my house
F inding a good spot
A t the end of Africa
R unning in the sun
I n a hot place.

Elizabeth Hickman (7)
Bitterne Manor Primary School, Southampton

Lion's Den

L ions hunting for meat.
I t sleeps in the day.
O n the hill hunting.
N eeds water at night-time.
S how off all the time.

D ens are warm!
E very day is hot.
N eeds its family.

Elizabeth Brading (6)
Bitterne Manor Primary School, Southampton

My First Acrostic - Southern Counties

Monkey Den

M onkey den
O n safari monkeys live
N o hitting monkeys
K iller bad monkey
E ats food
Y ou should have a monkey

D onkeys like monkeys
E at bananas do monkeys
N ever notice monkeys.

Aleeza Mabood (7)
Bitterne Manor Primary School, Southampton

Monkeys

M onkeys swing from vine to vine
O n the trees the monkey sits
N aughty monkey drops banana skins
K icking things about
E ating fruit and fleas
Y ahoo, this is fun
S wings from tree to tree!

Heather Brennan (6)
Bitterne Manor Primary School, Southampton

My First Acrostic - Southern Counties

On Safari

O n safari there are wild animals
N agging at each other

S nakes slithering
A cross the floor, rattling along the park
F inding their prey
A long the way
R unning away from predators
I n the safari park.

Darren Sutherland (7)
Bitterne Manor Primary School, Southampton

Snake Pit

S nakes are dangerous.
N ipping food.
A re very poisonous.
K icking things.
E ating their prey.

P icking sand up.
I t's found some food.
T rying their prey.

Thomas Dawson (7)
Bitterne Manor Primary School, Southampton

My First Acrostic - Southern Counties

Tiger

T igers like to eat meat.
I n the den the tiger sleeps.
G rowling tigers in their den.
E ating meat.
R oars in its den.

Beth Berman-Hughes (7)
Bitterne Manor Primary School, Southampton

Monkey

M onkeys eat fleas.
O n the tree they swing.
N o work.
K eep on the ground.
E at bananas.
Y es, they swing.

Rueben Whitehead (7)
Bitterne Manor Primary School, Southampton

My First Acrostic - Southern Counties

Lion's Den

L ight lion
I t lays on hay
O n the hills
N obody goes to see lions

D ens are for lions, not you
E mus don't go near lions
N o you won't go in there.

Abigail Page (7)
Bitterne Manor Primary School, Southampton

Leopards

L eopards climbing trees
E ating monkeys
O ver a hill chasing you!
P art of the cat family
A ngry because of tigers eating their food
R eally scary
D aily sleeping
S cary as can be!

Jasmine Sainsbury (7)
Bitterne Manor Primary School, Southampton

My First Acrostic - Southern Counties

Tiger

T iger can see prey.

I t finds meat to eat.

'G rowl,' said the tiger, 'I want some food.'
said the tiger, 'I want some food.'

E very day the tigers hunt for food.

R ed and black stripes.

Riley Whitehead
Bitterne Manor Primary School, Southampton

Gorilla

G iant gorilla
O range eater
R unner
I gloo hunter
L ong jumper
L ong legs
A climber.

Gian Chahal (7)
Bitterne Manor Primary School, Southampton

My First Acrostic - Southern Counties

Africa

A nice sunny day outside Africa.

F rom a spotlight shade.

R ows of people searching, buying, waving, saying goodbye.

I t is always hot in Africa when the sun's out.

C urling up, saying goodnight, you sleep in a tent.

A cool day would be nice for all.

Brooke Lewis (7)
Bitterne Manor Primary School, Southampton

An Acrostic Poem About Me

I am seven and a half.

September is my birthday.

Oxfordshire is where I live.

Bright and good.

Expert at science.

Leopards are my favourite animal.

Terrific at studying dinosaurs.

Arty and creative.

Yoghurts are yummy.

Lovely and polite.

October is my best friend, Jack's, birthday.

Reading books is great!

Isobel Taylor (7)
Chalgrove School, Chalgrove

An Acrostic Poem About Me

H appy all the time.
O xford is where I like to go shopping.
L ovely and nice.
L ike going to my swimming lesson.
Y ummy apples are the best.

C halgrove is where I live.
R eading my favourite fairy books.
O ctober is my teacher's birthday.
S eptember the seventh is my birthday.
T he month of Megan's birthday is December.
H ealthy girl.
W ill go to the park with Mummy.
A ugust is my daddy's birthday.
I am 6 and 3 quarters.
T he month of my mummy's birthday is May.
E ating sweets and chocolate are my favourite foods.

Holly Crosthwaite (6)
Chalgrove School, Chalgrove

An Acrostic Poem About Me

C razy like a cheetah.
O lives are disgusting.
N eat writing.
N ever tidy is my room.
O xford is where I live.
R eading books is fun.

C heeky person.
A rtistic boy.
F avourite food is pizza.
F unny fellow.
E at chocolate all the time.
L azy when I get up.

Connor Caffel (7)
Chalgrove School, Chalgrove

My First Acrostic - Southern Counties

An Acrostic Poem About Me

T om is nice and kind.
O ctober is my birthday.
M y brother and sisters are called Joe, Sophy and Elly.

M y favourite food is cake.
E arly for school is important.
R ace very fast.
C ooking is fun!
E xcellent footballer.
R unning at break time with my friends.

Tom Mercer (6)
Chalgrove School, Chalgrove

An Acrostic Poem About Me

C aring
I ce cream
A thletic
R ight
A pples

R unning
O xfordshire
G orgeous
E nergetic
R ock girl
S untanned.

Ciara Rogers (7)
Chalgrove School, Chalgrove

An Acrostic Poem About Me

K een
E xciting
R eliable
A rtistic

B eautiful
A fraid
K ind
E xcitable
R eads.

Kera Baker (7)
Chalgrove School, Chalgrove

An Acrostic Poem About Me

B ouncy
E xcited
A rtist
T icklish
R eader
I nteresting
C ute
E nergetic.

J umping
U nderstanding
S wims
T alkative
I maginative
C ares
E legant.

Beatrice Justice (6)
Chalgrove School, Chalgrove

My First Acrostic - Southern Counties

An Acrostic Poem About Me

O xford
L oveable
I ntelligent
V olunteer
I ndependent
A rtistic

S ix
O utstanding
P erfect
E njoy
R unning.

Olivia Soper (6)
Chalgrove School, Chalgrove

An Acrostic Poem About Me

T error
H elpful
O riginal
M usical
A ngry
S unny

M essy
A thletic
R eliable
R eads
I nteresting
A rtistic
G olfer
E xcitable.

Thomas Marriage (7)
Chalgrove School, Chalgrove

My First Acrostic - Southern Counties

An Acrostic Poem About Me

T he best colours are purple and yellow.
H ome is Chalgrove with Dad, Mum and Verity.
O ctober is my teacher's birthday.
M y best programme is Ben 10.
A rty and crafty.
S lithery under my bed.

H appy is how I feel.
A ustralia was my holiday.
R eally like animals.
R un fast around the playground.
I am polite.
S cared of the dark
O xford is near where I live.
N ot usual because sometimes I act like a dog.

Thomas Harrison (6)
Chalgrove School, Chalgrove

William Fern

W atch Ben 10 with my friends.
I like lions.
L oving and caring.
L ive in Oxfordshire, in a small village.
I love space and learning about planets and stars.
A nnoying things are seat belts.
M ay is when my birthday is.

F abulous Fern is my surname.
E at pizza, it's yummy, especially pepperoni.
R eading puzzle books is fun!
N umbers are brilliant.

William Fern (7)
Chalgrove School, Chalgrove

My First Acrostic - Southern Counties

Charlotte Arnold

C aring.
H appy.
A pples.
R ight.
L ovely.
O xfordshire.
T idy.
T ears.
E nergetic.

A thletic.
R ock girl.
N ice.
O ctober.
L oving.
D ancer.

Charlotte Arnold (6)
Chalgrove School, Chalgrove

An Acrostic Poem About Me

K een

Y awns

L ovely

E xcited

W orks hard

A thletic

T ig is my favourite game

T igers are the best animal

S porty.

Kyle Watts (7)
Chalgrove School, Chalgrove

My First Acrostic - Southern Counties

An Acrostic Poem About Me

M usical
I nterested
A rtistic

R osie
I maginative
C hocolate
H appy
A musing
R ealistic
D ifferent
S unny
O xford
N agger.

Mia Richardson (7)
Chalgrove School, Chalgrove

An Acrostic Poem About Me

C heesy feet man.

H appy and cheeky personality.

A rtistic.

R eally good at football and running.

L ovely little boy.

I have the best teacher in the world.

E at pizza, my favourite topping is pepperoni.

S mith is my surname.

M y favourite programme is Ben 10.

I like Lego, I can build lots of things.

T V is the best.

H angman is my favourite game.

Charlie Smith (7)
Chalgrove School, Chalgrove

An Acrostic Poem About Me

K ind
I nteresting
E xcitable
R eliable
A rtistic
N ice

L aughs
A thletic
W illing.

Kieran Law (6)
Chalgrove School, Chalgrove

An Acrostic Poem About Me

N eat handwriting.

A rtistic at painting.

O ctober is Miss Mullen's and Ciara's birthday.

M y horse is called Cheeky Charlie.

I love making igloos because it's fun.

F avourite animals are zebras and horses.

O xfordshire is where I live.

R eading animal books is great.

S hipton Under Wychwood is my other home.

Y ummy food is macaroni cheese.

T he best thing of all are animals.

H as five horses, two cats, two rabbits and one hamster.

Naomi Forsyth (7)
Chalgrove School, Chalgrove

My First Acrostic - Southern Counties

An Acrostic Poem About Me

J ack is a joyful boy and October is my birthday.
A fraid of the dark.
C areful at homework.
K icking a football is fun.

C urious about science.
A chy ears sometimes hurt me.
R uns well and loves athletics.
T ricks brilliantly!
E ats yummy food like cheese and pasta.
R eads interesting books about dinosaurs.

Jack Carter (6)
Chalgrove School, Chalgrove

An Acrostic Poem About Me

C ute girl.

H appy and cheerful.

A pple eater, they are delicious.

R osy cheeks from running around.

L ovely and pretty.

O xford is my favourite place.

T oothy person.

T he best TV programme is 'Britain's Got Talent'.

E nergetic person.

G lamorous and gorgeous.

R eally good at literacy.

E nergetic person.

H orses are my best animal.

A ct like an elephant.

N aughty and sneaky sometimes.

Charlotte Grehan (7)
Chalgrove School, Chalgrove

An Acrostic Poem About Me

H airy handsome boy.
A pples are my break time snack.
R eally good at football.
R unning at playtime with my friends.
I ce cream is my favourite food.
S ix years old is my age.
O ctober is my teacher's birthday.
N aughty sometimes.

T he best TV programme is 'Britain's Got Talent'.
O xford United are my best football team.
D iving in swimming pool.
D rink lots of orange squash.

Harrison Todd (6)
Chalgrove School, Chalgrove

An Acrostic Poem About Me

M y favourite colour is purple.
I 've got a sister called Mailyah and a brother called Myles.
A ugust is my birthday month.

M y favourite jam is plum.
O ften play with my friend Bea.
O xford is my home city.
R ock pools are fun, they are warm.
E ating pizza is yummy.
S hells are my best thing.

Mia Moores (6)
Chalgrove School, Chalgrove

My First Acrostic - Southern Counties

Myself

C razy when I see chocolate bars.

O ctopuses in the ocean are my favourite sea creatures.

N ice when playing with my friends.

R atbag when naughty at home.

A nts are naughty.

D elicious pizza as a Friday treat.

Conrad Peck (6)
Combe CE Primary School, Witney

Myself

J umpy when I am jumping on the terrific trampoline.
O utstanding at adding in maths.
S urprising like a naughty ninja.
H ilarious when I tell a joyful joke.

Josh Stares (7)
Combe CE Primary School, Witney

My First Acrostic - Southern Counties

Myself

A nts are my favourite insects.
X ylophones are lovely to listen to.
E xcellent at English.
L oud when I am in the playground.

Axel Stares (6)
Combe CE Primary School, Witney

Myself

J ust so good at climbing trees.

O ctopuses are lovely sea creatures.

S uper at attacking my brother.

E xcellent at eating eggs.

P ercy the prefect is very funny.

H arry Potter is my favourite character.

Joseph Creasey (6)
Combe CE Primary School, Witney

My First Acrostic - Southern Counties

Myself

A pples are my favourite food.
I adore scaly, slippery snakes.
D angerous dinosaurs are my favourite species.
A nts are little monkeys when they crawl on my leg.
N ever been naughty at school.

Aidan Paterson (6)
Combe CE Primary School, Witney

Myself

Great at reading my favourite books.

Excellent at football.

Orange juice squirts in my eye as I eat.

Ripe apples I like to eat.

Games are good to play especially Mousetrap.

Energetic around the playground.

George Bugler (7)
Combe CE Primary School, Witney

My First Acrostic - Southern Counties

Myself

B eautiful at parties in my sparkly dresses.
E xcellent at maths.
T alented at dancing to pop music.
H appy when I'm visiting new places.
A rt is fun.
N ice to little children.
Y es, I'm great at cheering people up.

Bethany Paine (6)
Combe CE Primary School, Witney

Myself

O utstanding me adores Mrs Pascoe.
L ovely little Tilly is my special sister.
I am interested in tennis.
V ictoria is my fabulous French teacher.
I love delicious strawberry ice cream.
A pples I adore, they are green and juicy.

Olivia Westbrook (7)
Combe CE Primary School, Witney

My First Acrostic - Southern Counties

Myself

H annah is hard-working.

A pples are good for me.

N ice nail polish is pretty on my fingers and toes.

N aughty Nana gives me too many pressies.

A dorable leopards I think are cute.

H appy Hannah is cheerful on sunny days.

Hannah Sheppard (6)
Combe CE Primary School, Witney

Myself

M ummy loves me.

A lways like yummy pasta.

T he juicy red apples are my favourite fruit.

I love Isobel.

L ollipops are my favourite treat.

D addy makes pancakes.

A dorable cats are my favourite pets.

Matilda Bugler (6)
Combe CE Primary School, Witney

My First Acrostic - Southern Counties

Myself

C razy about football.
O utstanding at being the troll in the play.
N ice at playtime to my fabulous friends.
N aughty, noisy Isobel, my sister, is starting school.
O ctopus are my favourite sea creatures.
R ed kites swooping high are my favourite birds of prey.

Connor Kirby (7)
Combe CE Primary School, Witney

Myself

I sobel is incredibly intelligent like Mrs Pascoe.
S uper speller with sound reading helping me spell.
O ctagons are my favourite shape.
B eautiful smile as bright as the sun.
E xcellent at English.
L ovely like an angel.

Isobel Shone (7)
Combe CE Primary School, Witney

Myself

G orgeous when I'm smiling.
E xcellent at maths.
O ranges are my favourite fruit.
R ed is my favourite colour.
G irls I love.
I love Isobel and Jessie.
A lways playing with Barbies.

Georgia Nicholson (6)
Combe CE Primary School, Witney

Isla

I am impossible at making my bed.
Six years old I am.
Lovely blue eyes that sparkle in the shining sun.
Art is my favourite thing in school.

Isla Henderson (6)
Combe CE Primary School, Witney

My First Acrostic - Southern Counties

Myself

E legant I am when it comes to dancing.

L ovely me likes my friends.

L ucky me gets lots of presents for being good.

A nna likes me and I like her, she is my best Year 6 friend.

Ella Evans (7)
Combe CE Primary School, Witney

Myself

M arvellous me makes swimming fun.

I ce cream is my favourite fabulous food.

L ovely long leggings I have.

L ucky, lovely, long hair that is shiny and smooth.

I sobel is interesting and she is my friend.

E xcited, elegant Ella and I love to dance.

Millie Blakesley-Grimes (7)
Combe CE Primary School, Witney

My First Acrostic - Southern Counties

Swimming

S wimming is great fun for me.
W e are in a swimming group, in the middle of the pool.
I can swim very fast from one side to the other.
M y teacher is called Heather.
M y friends are in my group.
I am a confident swimmer.
N ow we are going on our last swim.
G etting good at my swimming.

Thomas Greatwood (7)
Forest & Sandridge CE Primary School, Melksham

Animals

A nimals are my favourite thing.
N ecks are long on giraffes.
I like the elephants, the best are fast.
M assive animals are slow and little animals.
A nimals are clever.
L ittle animals are cute.
S ome animals are big, some are little.

Joseph White (7)
Forest & Sandridge CE Primary School, Melksham

My First Acrostic - Southern Counties

Weymouth

W e like Weymouth.

E verybody likes the beach.

Y ou are good at swimming.

M y ice cream is minty.

O ctober I went to Weymouth.

U p the stairs to get to my bedroom.

T axis took me there.

H olidays are fun.

Casey Herron (7)
Forest & Sandridge CE Primary School, Melksham

Sports Day

S itting on the tyre is fun.
P laying, trying to win the race.
O i! Stop pushing me.
R elay is fun, it is my favourite.
T rying to do relay.
S aying I can do it.

D oing relay is so much fun.
A ll the Reds have won.
Y elling mums and dads.

Freya Wyatt (7)
Forest & Sandridge CE Primary School, Melksham

My First Acrostic - Southern Counties

Owen

O wen is my name.
W hen I play with my friends they say thank you.
E ggs are my favourite food.
N ewspapers are the best.

Owen Wood (7)
Forest & Sandridge CE Primary School, Melksham

Swimming

S wimming is so much fun.
W e are the best group.
I really like swimming.
M y group is the best.
M y group is the best at testing.
I go swimming every day.
N o one is a better swimmer than me.
G oing swimming is so much fun.

Tye Sullivan (7)
Forest & Sandridge CE Primary School, Melksham

My First Acrostic - Southern Counties

Swimming

S wimming makes you all wet.

W hen you are wet it feels great.

I got tested last week, it was hard.

M y group is group one and I go swimming first.

M y group has twelve people in it.

I think that we are the best.

N othing is bad about swimming because I like swimming.

G ood swimming is very healthy for you.

Brandon Humphries (7)
Forest & Sandridge CE Primary School, Melksham

Swimming

S wimming is so much fun
W e go every Tuesday
I like swimming
M y group is the best at testing
M y group is the best
I t is fun, swimming
N o one can beat me
G oing to swimming is fun.

Brendan Harvey (7)
Forest & Sandridge CE Primary School, Melksham

My First Acrostic - Southern Counties

Eloise

E loise is my name.
L iteracy is my favourite topic.
O n my own it is peaceful.
I like DT because making things is fun.
S ome objects are my favourite.
E lephants are my favourite animals.

Eloise Hatfield (7)
Forest & Sandridge CE Primary School, Melksham

Michael

My name is Michael.

I have brown eyes.

Cars are my favourite toys.

Home is my favourite place.

A dog is my favourite animal.

Everybody is my friend.

Luke is my brother.

Michael Wilkins (7)
Forest & Sandridge CE Primary School, Melksham

My First Acrostic - Southern Counties

Swimming

S wimming is really fun.
W ater helps you swim.
I love the water.
M elksham is the best.
M elksham pool is the best.
I go underwater at the blue pool in Melksham.
N ext we go back to school.
G etting in the pool, it is really cold in there.

Amy Vines (7)
Forest & Sandridge CE Primary School, Melksham

Isobel

I 'm nice and kind.
S cott is my best friend, he loves playing dogs.
O wen is my best friend too.
B ut Ben loves playing all the games we think of with me.
E loise is my best friend ever.
L ouise is my middle name.

Isobel Godsell (7)
Forest & Sandridge CE Primary School, Melksham

My First Acrostic - Southern Counties

Minibeasts

M y favourite minibeast is a woodlouse.
I like minibeasts a lot.
N ice minibeasts are my favourite.
I find the most minibeasts under rocks.
B y the log I found a long earwig.
E arwigs are quite long and they have long antennae.
A nts are very small, some are black and some are red.
S ometimes I find minibeasts in the grass.
T here's one minibeast that I don't like and it's a slimy slug.
S nails have lovely shells that usually have patterns on them.

Chloe Bowden (7)
Forest & Sandridge CE Primary School, Melksham

Paige

P aige loves to play.

A m a nice girl.

I like games.

G irls are fun to play with.

E verybody is nice to me.

Paige Charman (7)
Forest & Sandridge CE Primary School, Melksham

My First Acrostic - Southern Counties

Swimming

S wimming is fun.
W illow goes swimming.
I love swimming.
M y friend is good at swimming.
M rs Fountain takes us swimming.
I go swimming on Saturdays.
N ext week we don't go swimming.
G reat fun splashing in the water.

Evie Fish (6)
Forest & Sandridge CE Primary School, Melksham

Swimming

S wimming is fun.

W illow goes swimming every Tuesday.

I like going swimming.

M y friends are good at swimming.

M rs Fountain takes us swimming.

I go swimming on a Monday as well.

N ext week we don't go swimming because it has ended for this class.

G ood swimmers move up a stage.

Max Bramley (7)
Forest & Sandridge CE Primary School, Melksham

My First Acrostic - Southern Counties

Weymouth

W e like Weymouth.

E nd of the day we would go to the arcade.

Y ou would like to go to Weymouth.

M ummy went to the shop to buy sherbet.

O n Friday we went into the shop.

U sually we go to the game shop.

T axis would come get us.

H olidays are fun.

Milly Bannister (6)
Forest & Sandridge CE Primary School, Melksham

Scott

S cott is very, very kind.
C an you help Scott please?
O nce you've done, can you help me?
T ake this as a special present.
T omorrow do you want to play with me?

Scott Atkins (7)
Forest & Sandridge CE Primary School, Melksham

My First Acrostic - Southern Counties

Richard

R ichard is a cute and funny boy.
I have a gap in my teeth.
C ats are my favourite pets.
H am is my favourite sandwich
A nd I have blue eyes.
R ichard looks like his brother.
D ogs are his favourite pet.

Richard Andrews (7)
Forest & Sandridge CE Primary School, Melksham

Lucas Soedring

L ovely learner who is nice
U nusual person who is good
C lever worker who's good at maths
A wesome
S ilver trousers

S hares stuff
O nly nice but not naughty
E nergetic
D irected
R eally strict but only sometimes
I like ice cream
N ice
G ood.

Lucas Soedring (7)
Harestock Primary School, Winchester

My First Acrostic - Southern Counties

Adam Fisher

A wesome boy who is fun and nice
D efinitely this boy is an
A wesome boy
M akes people laugh

F riendly boy
I went on holiday to a far away place
S ilver trousers are my favourite
H e's always friendly
E veryone's friend
R eliable.

Adam Fisher
Harestock Primary School, Winchester

Mieszko

M athematical
I live a bit
E ager a bit
S uper special
Z appy and cool
K icker at football
O utstandingly funny.

Mieszko Stabolepszy (7)
Harestock Primary School, Winchester

My First Acrostic - Southern Counties

Oliver Hayes

O riginal person
L ovely boy
I mportant child
V aluable kid
E xcitable child
R ich mum

H orse rider
A mazing kid
Y ear 2
E ats bits of food
S wimmer.

Oliver Hayes
Harestock Primary School, Winchester

Laura

L ovely to everyone!
A ctive and fit.
U nicorns are the best.
R eally fun.
A mazing at karate.

Laura Soper (7)
Harestock Primary School, Winchester

My First Acrostic - Southern Counties

Michael

M anly
I like football
C ool person
H elpful to others
A ctive
E ntertaining
L ikeable.

Michael George (7)
Harestock Primary School, Winchester

Matthew

M athematical person
A ccurate and active
T ennis is one of my favourite sports
T remendous
H appy and fit
E ager
W orkable.

Matthew Hoyland (7)
Harestock Primary School, Winchester

My First Acrostic - Southern Counties

Maisie Stead

M arvellous
A ddicted to 'High School Musical'
I nteresting
S illy
I ndependent
E xcitable

S teady
T alkative
E ntertainer
A mazing
D iddy.

Maisie Stead
Harestock Primary School, Winchester

Ryan

R eally clever.
Y ellow hair.
A cts good at lunchtime and play.
N ice most of the time.

Ryan Barker (7)
Harestock Primary School, Winchester

My First Acrostic - Southern Counties

Abbie

A nice person
B ubbly girl
B ee lover
I love ice cream
E gg eater.

Abbie Hamilton (7)
Harestock Primary School, Winchester

Amber

A bright girl
My interests are monkeys
Bumblebees sting me
Eyes are interestingly cool
Really pretty.

Amber Mears
Harestock Primary School, Winchester

My First Acrostic - Southern Counties

Lily Smithers

L ovely
I mpressive
L oveable
Y oung

S miley
M agical
I nteresting
T alkative
H appy
E xciting
R uns
S kips.

Lily Smithers (7)
Harestock Primary School, Winchester

Kitty

K ind and clever
I nterested in animals
T rue
T iny
Y oghurt lover.

Kitty Chappell (6)
Harestock Primary School, Winchester

My First Acrostic - Southern Counties

Summer

S parkling meadows shimmering in the sunlight.

U nicorn shadows galloping everywhere.

M ysterious creatures crawling round in circles.

M onth by month we wait for the summer, when it comes there's lots to discover.

E ager children start races on sunny sports day.

R ed roses being planted in lovely green fields.

Charlotte McDowall (7)
Highnam Primary School, Highnam

Italy

I like Leonardo da Vinci's paintings.
The lady called Mona Lisa was from Italy.
An aeroplane is made by Leonardo da Vinci.
Leaning Tower of Pisa is in Italy.
You can eat a pizza in Italy.

Swathan Meenakumar (7)
Longleaze Primary School, Swindon

My First Acrostic - Southern Counties

Italy

I like pizza.

The Leaning Tower of Pisa.

Aeroplanes were invented by Leonardo da Vinci.

Leonardo da Vinci was a painter.

You can eat a sausage in Italy.

Max Hopkins (6)
Longleaze Primary School, Swindon

Italy

I love learning how to make pizza.
T he Leaning Tower of Pisa.
A man painted the Mona Lisa.
L eonardo da Vinci.
Y ou can fly to Italy.

Megan Lockett & Charlie Lambert (6)
Longleaze Primary School, Swindon

Italy

I like the Mona Lisa
T he pizza is yummy
A person called Leonardo da Vinci
L eonardo da Vinci was an artist
Y ou can visit the Leaning Tower of Pisa.

Pheobe Doe (6)
Longleaze Primary School, Swindon

Italy

I n Italy I can see Pisa

T he Leaning Tower is in Pisa

A eroplanes can fly

L eonardo da Vinci painted lots of pictures

Y ou can eat pizza in Italy.

Thea Hopkins (6)
Longleaze Primary School, Swindon

My First Acrostic - Southern Counties

Billy

B illy is fun to play with
I like playing
L ove football
L ove my dinner
Y oghurts are my least favourite food.

Billy Smith (6)
Medina Primary School, Cosham

Puppies

P eople take them

U nder some trees

P uppies lay down

P retty, playing fools

Y oung puppies stay inside.

Daisy-May English (5)
Medina Primary School, Cosham

My First Acrostic - Southern Counties

School

S neaky head teacher
C up of tea
H ard work
O range flowers
O utside having fun
L ots of things to do.

Jayden Ridout (6)
Medina Primary School, Cosham

Mrs Barker

M rs Barker is pretty
R eally friendly
S oft

B lue
A tall girl
R emember good things
K ind
E verything looks nice on you
R eally gorgeous.

Hannah Goodwin (6)
Medina Primary School, Cosham

My First Acrostic - Southern Counties

Ryan

R yan is my best friend
Y ou are very nice
A nd you are brilliant at Ben 10
N o one is better than you at Ben 10.

Kai Passingham-Hutchings (5)
Medina Primary School, Cosham

Tanks

T anks are big
A tank is powerful
N o one can defeat
K ing-sized tanks
S ome tanks are so fast they can speed across water.

Jack Goodwin (6)
Medina Primary School, Cosham

My First Acrostic - Southern Counties

Food

F ood at breakfast
O range on the side
O range juice in a cup
D on't eat the orange skin!

Ryan Armstrong (6)
Medina Primary School, Cosham

Cars

C ars are clever.
A car is a good car.
R acing cars are the best.
S ome cars are terrific.

Cain Wallace (6)
Medina Primary School, Cosham

My First Acrostic - Southern Counties

Chocolate

C hocolate is yum
H appy
O range
C ake
O blong
L ovely
A eros
T asty
E nergy, because I have some!

Nivara Gregory (6)
Medina Primary School, Cosham

Flowers

F lowers are beautiful, there are lots of different flowers.
L ittle flowers are really nice.
O range flowers.
W hite daisies.
E very flower has nectar.
R ed flowers are roses.
S un makes flowers grow.

Tulula Romer (6)
Medina Primary School, Cosham

My First Acrostic - Southern Counties

House

H ouse is a home.
O ne house I've got.
U mbrella lives in house.
S ome houses are old.
E very day people build houses.

Keeley Newell (6)
Medina Primary School, Cosham

Flowers

F lowers smell lovely
L ight colours
O range flowers
W hite flowers
E very flower has pollen
R ed flowers are roses
S unflowers.

Archie Drury (6)
Medina Primary School, Cosham

My First Acrostic - Southern Counties

Jimmy

J immy is fun
I like ice lollies
M e and my sister race
M y favourite time is me time
Y oghurts are my favourite things to eat.

Jimmy Cook (6)
Medina Primary School, Cosham

Dad

D ads are great
A dad is always burping
D ads run everywhere.

Shannon-Marie Harvell (6)
Medina Primary School, Cosham

My First Acrostic - Southern Counties

Daniela

D aisy-May is nice
A nna is beautiful
N ivara is nice
I ncredible
E gg
L illy
A ngela.

Daniela Monen (6)
Medina Primary School, Cosham

Finlay

F earless and funky, I like to play football
I also like watching TV and films
N ice and helpful I like to be
L iving in a good sized house
A dventurous I like to be
Y ou might like me.

Finlay Hawkins (7)
Meysey Hampton CE Primary School, Cirencester

My First Acrostic - Southern Counties

Miles

M arvellous playing in the sun with his friends
I nventing Miles working very hard inside
L ittle Miles living in a house
E xciting Miles having lunch
S illy Miles is very funny.

Miles Farrington (7)
Meysey Hampton CE Primary School, Cirencester

Ashley

A pples are my favourite fruit
S oon I will hug a puppy
H er name will be Bailey
L ater I will love the puppy
E veryone will love the puppy
Y ou can come and see the puppy.

Ashley Stutzman (7)
Meysey Hampton CE Primary School, Cirencester

My First Acrostic - Southern Counties

Jos

J ogging Jos goes out for a jog after that she goes to the garden to do her

O bstacle course and it is very new, she bought it on Sunday,

S upper was ready for her so she went inside to have her supper.

Joscelyn Moore (6)
Meysey Hampton CE Primary School, Cirencester

Patrick

P atrick is a boy
A funny, cute boy
T oo smiley to be true
R eady forever
I n my house
C hristmas is my favourite time of year
K eep out of the way, I can be quite frightening.

Patrick Wright (6)
Meysey Hampton CE Primary School, Cirencester

My First Acrostic - Southern Counties

Natasha

N ever selfish at playtime
A mazing at skipping
T icklish all over
A lways eating apples
S inging at playtime
H urrying to my mummy
A sleep in my bed.

Natasha Gleeson (6)
Meysey Hampton CE Primary School, Cirencester

Joshua

J oshua likes jelly
O ften I go to school
S peedy trains I love
H am sandwiches I like for lunch
U nderground I play with my trains
A nimals are my friends.

Joshua Mason (6)
Meysey Hampton CE Primary School, Cirencester

My First Acrostic - Southern Counties

Poppy

P ink is my favourite colour
O utside is where I like to be
P laying is what I like to do
P arties I love to go to
Y ellow I like a bit too!

Poppy Nicholls (7)
Meysey Hampton CE Primary School, Cirencester

Molly

M y best colour is green
O lly is my best friend
L ovely Molly, nice and sweet
L ittle lovely Molly
Y esterday Molly went shopping.

Molly Davies (6)
Meysey Hampton CE Primary School, Cirencester

My First Acrostic - Southern Counties

David

D avid is a dad that knows everything
A t the park I go on the swing with David
V ery impressive handstands, he can do
I n the house he plays board games with me
D id you know that David is a very good climber.

Alex Finnegan (6)
Meysey Hampton CE Primary School, Cirencester

Jamie

J amie likes going to Tesco
A sandwich is my best lunch
M y mum likes playing with me and making me happy
I like going to the park
E veryone likes playing with me.

Jamie Whitehouse (6)
Meysey Hampton CE Primary School, Cirencester

My First Acrostic - Southern Counties

Seaside

S eagulls flying, swooping and swaying along the beach on a sunny day
E very day people play in the sea
A long the beach my friends play with me
S lipping and sliding in the bay
I n the sea on a sunny day
D oing nothing in the sun
E ating an ice cream, having fun.

Katie Jarvey (6)
Millbrook Primary School, Wantage

Crab

C rabs pinch
R ug for sitting on
A ll sorts of food
B ring lots of suncream.

Sam Cheshire (6)
Millbrook Primary School, Wantage

My First Acrostic - Southern Counties

Sea

S eagulls flying
E verywhere
A long the water.

Amy Simcock (6)
Millbrook Primary School, Wantage

Sea

S eagulls
E at fish
A nd they dive.

Dylan Drake (6)
Millbrook Primary School, Wantage

Sea

S ea is fun

E verybody has fun swimming

A nd in the sea watch out, crabs might nibble your toes!

Sophie Jones (6)
Millbrook Primary School, Wantage

Sea

S eagulls flying
E ast and north
A long the beach.

Emily McArdle (6)
Millbrook Primary School, Wantage

My First Acrostic - Southern Counties

Sea

S and
E verywhere
A nd tickling my toes.

Michael Hollier (6)
Millbrook Primary School, Wantage

Henley

H appy girl
E xcited person
N ice girl
L ovely and caring
E xcellent in every way
Y oghurt is my favourite food.

Clara Henley (6)
Newton Tony CE Primary School, Salisbury

My First Acrostic - Southern Counties

Luke's Poem

H ealthy and strong boy
O utstanding at reading
U seful and good-looking
G ood and grown-up boy
H elpful and marvellous
T all and great
O bedient big boy
N ever naughty.

Luke Houghton (7)
Newton Tony CE Primary School, Salisbury

Sea Life

S alty water is a house for a dolphin.
E els wiggle like a green snake.
A mazing sea horses swimming up and down.

L ittle fish swimming up and down.
I cy, shiny water sailing around.
F ierce sharks biting children.
E normous whales singing in the sparkling water.

Madina Islam
St George's Beneficial School, Portsmouth

My First Acrostic - Southern Counties

Sea Life

S alty water all the time.
E lectric eels glowing in the shadows.
A mazing dolphins swimming with their babies.

L ost pearls in an oyster shell.
I nteresting octopus squirting ink everywhere.
F ish laying eggs in seaweed.
E xcited clownfish ready to do some tricks.

Laura Coombes (7)
St George's Beneficial School, Portsmouth

Sea Life

S cared because you might drown.
E nergetic because sometimes it might be a big beach.
A mazing because you might see crabs and lovely sea.

L ovely and salty sea.
I ncredible you might get covered with sand.
F ish are incredible because they swim fast.
E xcited when you get there.

Owen Scrivens (7)
St George's Beneficial School, Portsmouth

My First Acrostic - Southern Counties

Sea Life

S wimming around the sea are fish.
E lectric eels hide in seaweed to catch food.
A nemones are waving gently in the currents.

L ittle sea horse are very tiny.
I ncredible, interesting, colourful fish.
F unny clownfish swimming around in the sea.
E normous shark whale with its huge mouth.

Felicity Walker
St George's Beneficial School, Portsmouth

Sea Life

S wimming quietly in the blue water.
E lectric eels like eating lovely beautiful fish.
A nemones like to eat microscopic plankton from the sea.

L ittle fish swim away from predators.
I ncredible clownfish are multicoloured.
F ish live in weeds.
E normous sharks eat lovely fish.

Owen Whiteaway (7)
St George's Beneficial School, Portsmouth

My First Acrostic - Southern Counties

Sea Life

S ea horses swim in the salty water.
E els are slimy in the water.
A mazing dolphins jump and curl.

L eaping whales make big waves.
I ncredible turtles surf on the waves.
F loppy bass fighting to get home.
E xcited prunes, unforeseen freeze.

Stan Griffin
St George's Beneficial School, Portsmouth

Sea Life

S alty water gave people salt.

E normous whale sharks look like whales.

A mazing sharks swim fast.

L eaping waves wet your toes.

I f you drink salty water you will be ill.

F loppy fish swim fast.

E lectric eels catch food quickly.

Rakan Alromayon (7)
St George's Beneficial School, Portsmouth

My First Acrostic - Southern Counties

Sea Life

S hells are on the land near the water.
E els live in the sea.
A nemones are sea creatures.

L ovely animals are in the sea.
I ncredible animals do bite.
F riendly animals don't bite.
E ager waves are big.

Logan Clark
St George's Beneficial School, Portsmouth

Sea Life

S alty seawater people swim in.
E ggs are hatching in the salty sea.
A nts digging under the sand.

L ollies on the ground.
I nk colours black as a cave.
F ish are colourful like the ocean.
E normous killer whale eating modem fish.

Chloe Cheshire (6)
St George's Beneficial School, Portsmouth

My First Acrostic - Southern Counties

Sea Life

S tarfish are beautiful and sticky.
E normous whale is swimming with her babies.
A mazing whales swimming in the sea.

L ittle baby fish eat nicely with their mum.
I ncredible things are red fish.
F loppy dolphin in the messy sea.
E normous fish in the sea, swimming in the messy sea.

Semilore Fagbola (7)
St George's Beneficial School, Portsmouth

What Benjamin Can Do

- **B** rilliant at throwing balls
- **E** ats broccoli and carrots
- **N** early got a brown belt down
- **J** umps really high
- **A** mazing at drawing castles
- **M** agnificent at playing football
- **I** nterested in Manchester United
- **N** early uses capital letters and full stops all of the time.

Benjamin Lolljowaheer (6)
St Jude's RC Primary School, Fareham

My First Acrostic - Southern Counties

Fantastic Francesca

F antastic at diving underwater.

R emembers to be polite.

A lways plays nicely with her friends.

N ever be nasty to her friends.

C areful at making her breakfast.

E ats her dinner all up.

S low at eating her dinner.

C lever at writing stories.

A mazing at doing handstands underwater.

Francesca Fryers (7)
St Jude's RC Primary School, Fareham

Reading Reuben

R eads very loudly so everyone can hear him.
E ats very nicely so everyone in his house copies him.
U sually good at maths, that is why he is in the pentagons group.
B est at climbing really big ladders.
E very day he wants to go to school.
N ever eats big broccoli.

Reuben Menezes (6)
St Jude's RC Primary School, Fareham

My First Acrostic - Southern Counties

Merry Moyo

M agnificent at joining her letters when doing writing.
O ften silly when playing with Rithka on the field.
Y ells at Tope when she's annoying.
O wns a blue bike.

O nly has one sister.
D irty whenever she spills her food.
U nderstands her daddy whenever he speaks.
D own whenever she's lonely.
E xcited whenever she's happy.

Moyo Odude (7)
St Jude's RC Primary School, Fareham

About Tom

T all and has big feet
H oping for a DSI game
O nly goes to his nan's on Sunday
M isses his friends at the weekend
A mazing at karate
S leeps every day.

Thomas Wylde (7)
St Jude's RC Primary School, Fareham

My First Acrostic - Southern Counties

Tough Tom!

T errible at fighting with his brother
O nly eats roast dinners on Sundays
M ust tidy his bedroom every Monday

B rilliant at sport
R eally good at running fast
U sually likes playing football
C an race very fast
E asily comes first.

Thomas Bruce (7)
St Jude's RC Primary School, Fareham

Big Byron

Big and strong

Yellow is his favourite colour

Rocks with his guitar

Only goes out on Saturdays

Nearly built a car track with his bricks.

Byron Snook (7)
St Jude's RC Primary School, Fareham

My First Acrostic - Southern Counties

Happy Holly

H orse rides and jumps but never falls off
O ur pony is never naughty
L icks her lollipop a day long
L ies to her mum and dad all the time
Y ells to her sister all the time.

Holly Cristofoli (7)
St Jude's RC Primary School, Fareham

Dynamic Daniel

D rives a Porsche
A lways likes to play with his friends
N early can ride his bike
I s good at running
E ats noodles
L ikes boxing.

Daniel Chadwick (6)
St Jude's RC Primary School, Fareham

Alligator Andrew

A lways amazing at football and scoring great goals
N ever hates easy maths
D ries his washing does his mum
R ides his bike in the park
E ats vegetables and eats his fruit
W ild when he goes to bed.

Andrew Evans (7)
St Jude's RC Primary School, Fareham

All About Me

R emembers all his things for school
Y ells at his brother
A sks his mum for 50p to spend on sweets
N early got a goal in football.

Ryan Hockaday (7)
St Jude's RC Primary School, Fareham

My First Acrostic - Southern Counties

Fearless Finlay

F earlessly does a forward flip on his trampoline
I ncredibly fast at riding his bike at the park
N ever gets money without doing jobs at home
L oves playing pool with his dad every Saturday night
A lways gets a Beast Quest when he's done a good job at home
Y awns loudly every Monday morning.

Finlay Harrison (7)
St Jude's RC Primary School, Fareham

Excellent Emma

E xcellent at gymnastics, handstands and cartwheels
M akes fortune tellers and decorates them
M agnificent at drawing and colouring in
A mazing at horse riding and jumping over fences

B uys lots of food for her gerbils
O wns a big trampoline and can jump very high
L ives in a huge house and has a very big room
W ill always look after her pets and cares for them
E ats fish and chips on a Friday night
L ies on her bed and reads a book
L eads her pony into a big green field.

Emma Bolwell (6)
St Jude's RC Primary School, Fareham

My First Acrostic - Southern Counties

Amazing Emma

E ats everything on her plate when it is chicken pie
M agnificent at ballet, dancing and jumping very high
M ixes cake ingredients to help her mum and dad
A mazing at cartwheels and handstands on the school field

W ill always read her book
R eads her book nicely in the morning
I ncludes everyone in her games and helps people
                                             when they fall over
G ets to go to her nan's house every Friday for tea
H appy and smiles a lot
T errible at tidying her room.

Emma Wright (7)
St Jude's RC Primary School, Fareham

Lucky Lucas

L ucky and always wins
U sually is angry at his brother
C razy at football and rugby
A mazing at doing front and backflips
S leepy in the morning.

Lucas Miles (6)
St Jude's RC Primary School, Fareham

My First Acrostic - Southern Counties

Clever Fred

F erocious when he fights his big sister
R emembers to know his twos and fives table
E very day he plays football
D angerously picks up sticks and tries to hit his sister

H unts for fossils on the Isle of Wight
A mazing at diving and football
M agnificent at lots and lots of sports
I ncredible at running and playing football with his friends
L ikes doing lots of sports
T errible at maths and English
O utside loads of times with his friends
N ever remembers to get changed quickly for school.

Fred Hamilton (7)
St Jude's RC Primary School, Fareham

Tara Goes Mad

Takes care of poor animals and feeds them.
Always draws fantastic pictures of famous people.
Rides quickly in motor cars and on motorbikes.
Amazing at singing and dancing.

Makes clay models into masterpieces.
It's hard for her to hear my voice when I speak.
Sits on lumpy chairs and stools.
Kisses me when I go to bed.
Eats lots of food on Monday and Tuesday.
Lazy and sleepy most of the time.
Licks lollies when it's hot.
Angry and furious at me when I eat too many sweets.

Ciaran Miskella (7)
St Jude's RC Primary School, Fareham

My First Acrostic - Southern Counties

Fabulous Finn

F abulous at swimming on Thursdays
I ncredible at recognising dinosaurs, especially carnivores
N ormally goes for a picnic where there's brambles
N ever gets to go to the park to go on the swing.

Finn Judge (7)
St Jude's RC Primary School, Fareham

Lovely Libby

L ooks carefully at choosing what to wear
I s good at gymnastics
B eats people in races sometimes
B umps her head all the time
Y ells at her sister when she is at home.

Libby Choularton (7)
St Jude's RC Primary School, Fareham

My First Acrostic - Southern Counties

My Friend, Fast Tom

T elling is his favourite thing
O riginal at mixing when he makes a cake
M um always tells him off when he fights with his brother

B eats everyone in running races
R aces are awesome
U nderstands lots of maths
C an eat lots of vegetables every day
E ats lots of food.

Owen Joice (7)
St Jude's RC Primary School, Fareham

Crazy Carole

C razy about elephants and always talking about them.
A lways looking for jobs and things to do.
R ides a car called Daisy and it has flowers on the back of it.
O riginal at art work and cleaning.
L ovely at making speeches to other people.
E xtremely good at writing.

H orrible at singing and dancing.
U nderstanding when explaining something.
M agnificent at art, science and drawing.
P olite when eating and talking.
H orrid when angry.
R eally good at reading.
E xtremely good at baking bread.
Y ellow is her favourite colour.

Sophie-Jade Humphrey (7)
St Jude's RC Primary School, Fareham

My First Acrostic - Southern Counties

Super Sarah!

S uper fast at skipping.
A lways eats her dinner.
R oast is her favourite meal.
A mazing at maths.
H appy when she goes on holiday.

Sarah Collins (6)
St Jude's RC Primary School, Fareham

Lucy

L ucy sings in the dark by the moonlight.
U nderstands all the things she does.
C lean, cool Lucy hangs out with her mates.
Y oung Lucy is very brainy.

Hope Swain (7)
Standlake CE Primary School, Standlake

My First Acrostic - Southern Counties

Cars

C ars are noisy
A nd you never know where they go
R ound, round
S illy.

Joshua Gauntlett (6)
Standlake CE Primary School, Standlake

Josh B

J olly Josh B is six
O thers like him
S illy Josh is jolly
H elpful more than anybody

B ottle is always full of happy juice.

Will Ellett (6)
Standlake CE Primary School, Standlake

My First Acrostic - Southern Counties

Ice Cream

I gloo as cold as ice cream
C reamy hands
E xtremely yummy

C old and sticky
R ose-flavoured
E at it every day
A nd never let go
M ummy eats too much.

Jacob Denmark Fyfe (6)
Standlake CE Primary School, Standlake

Grace

Gorgeous Grace
Really kind to me
Always by my side
Caring and sharing
Eats fish finger pie.

Grace Soame (7)
Standlake CE Primary School, Standlake

My First Acrostic - Southern Counties

Meerkat

M e and Meerkat play all day.
E very day he helps me with my sums.
E very day when I'm at school he plays at home.
R avenous, running around the floor looking for food.
K icking is his weapon.
A lways eating bugs that is what he does.
T op gear in running is 100mph!

Josh Barber (6)
Standlake CE Primary School, Standlake

Mountain

M agical mountain way up high in the sky
O ld, old mountain, older than my granny
U p high in the sky
N o one can see as high as a mountain
T all, tall as can be
A ll the mountain snow is falling
I n the sky the mountain is touching the sky
N oisy all around.

Jonah King (6)
Standlake CE Primary School, Standlake

My First Acrostic - Southern Counties

Harry

H arry is a big fat cat
A lways sleeping on his chair
R ips up toys sometimes
R eally good at eating
Y et asleep again.

William Woodford (7)
Standlake CE Primary School, Standlake

Jamie

J olly Jamie
A lways works hard
M ates with William
I ntelligent sometimes
E xtremely helpful.

Jamie Beland (7)
Standlake CE Primary School, Standlake

My First Acrostic - Southern Counties

Sun

S un star is up high in the sky
U p high in space
N ice and yellow.

Becky Evans (6)
Standlake CE Primary School, Standlake

Ella

E legant Ella
L ovely and laughing Ella
L ucky and laughing
A lways helping and nice.

Morganna Swain (7)
Standlake CE Primary School, Standlake

My First Acrostic - Southern Counties

Ocean

O nly fish under the sea, swimming around as free as can be.

C lear water under the sea, as sparkly as can be.

E ach fish under the sea, clean and so colourful as can be.

A ll the fish in here are getting ready for a party.

N ice music with all the fish as happy as can be.

Savannah Willans (6)
Standlake CE Primary School, Standlake

My Daniel

D ad and me play tennis
A nd we play walk the dog
N ow it's night-time
I t's time for bed
E ven Charlotte too
L ove Mum and Dad.

Daniel Hobbs (6)
Stratford-Sub-Castle School, Salisbury

My First Acrostic - Southern Counties

My Friend

S adie is my best friend
C omes to my house to play
A game of dressing up
R un together on the field
L isten to each other
E ach of us likes the other
T ry to be kind to each other
T hink about each other.

Scarlett Cooper
Stratford-Sub-Castle School, Salisbury

The Seaside

S and gets in my sandwiches
E very time I go to the beach
A fter I go in the sea I have an ice cream
S wim in the sea with a friend
I make a sandcastle
D ive in the waves
E at lots of ice cream.

Gabrielle Ashton (7)
Stratford-Sub-Castle School, Salisbury

My Name

A lways eating apples
S he plays in the sunshine
H elps other people
L icks her lips
E njoys school
Y ou play with a yo-yo.

Ashley Nuccio (7)
Stratford-Sub-Castle School, Salisbury

My Name

S uper speller
A mazing footballer
M akes people happy
U nderstands everything
E asy to get on with
L ikes playing on the computer.

Samuel Webb (7)
Stratford-Sub-Castle School, Salisbury

My First Acrostic - Southern Counties

Seaside

C rawling crabs on the beach
R ock pools where starfish rest
A nd I found some shells, on the
B each are lots of sandcastles.

Russell Read (6)
Stratford-Sub-Castle School, Salisbury

Friends

S carlett is my friend
A lways run on the field
D ancing together
I n the evening
E ach of us share our photos.

Sadie Montgomery (7)
Stratford-Sub-Castle School, Salisbury

My First Acrostic - Southern Counties

Crab

C rawling crabs on the beach
R ock pools where starfish rest
A nd I found some shells
B each has lots of sandcastles.

Aliesha Hirang (6)
Stratford-Sub-Castle School, Salisbury

My Name

S hells are my favourite things
C at's name is Tigger
O utside playing with my toys
T aking my bike out
T o my aunty Lanas.

Scott Gray (7)
Stratford-Sub-Castle School, Salisbury

My First Acrostic - Southern Counties

My Dad

H e helps me to play football
A nd he makes me milkshakes
R eads me a story
V ery scary
E very night
Y ou are my dad.

Harvey Guilder (6)
Stratford-Sub-Castle School, Salisbury

My Name

H appy to be at school
A lways try to catch a fish in the lake
R abbit is my pet
R aspberries are my favourite fruit
Y et I like apples and oranges.

Harry Lewis (6)
Stratford-Sub-Castle School, Salisbury

My First Acrostic - Southern Counties

Sea

S and gets in my sandwiches
E very time I go to the beach it rains
A nd I always have an ice cream.

Fern Crumbie (5)
Stratford-Sub-Castle School, Salisbury

The Rainforest

R attlesnake slithering
A nts scuttle along
I nsects crawling
N ectar-eating insects
F lowers excellent
O rang-utan swing along the trees
R iver splashing
E xcited tiger
S nake hissing
T urtle walking along the ground.

Jack Coldrick (5)
The Grey House School, Hartley Wintney

The Rainforest

R unning in the rainforest, animals are sweet
A rattlesnake rattling its tail
I nsects marching away to fetch food
N oisy cockatoos squawking
F lowers are yellow and lots of lovely colours
O rang-utans swing from branch to branch
R ainforest animals are getting excited
E lephants trumpeting
S nakes slithering
T igers sleeping in the rainforest.

Clemmie Quilter-Wood (5)
The Grey House School, Hartley Wintney

The Rainforest

R ain falling through the trees
A chameleon climbing through the trees
I nteresting trees
N oises coming from the chameleons
F eet cracking through the leaves
O rang-utans swinging through the trees
R iver coming through the leaves
E lephants plodding through the trees
S tones falling through the waterfall
T oucans flying on top of the trees.

William Barnfield (5)
The Grey House School, Hartley Wintney

My First Acrostic - Southern Counties

The Rainforest

R attlesnakes go *rattle, rattle, rattle* and they go *slither, slither, slither*
A nts go *tap, tap, tap*
I nteresting animals go *tap, slither, rattle*
N ectar is collected by bees
F lowers grow lovely colours
O rang-utans swing from branch to branch
R abbits go *boing, boing, boing*
E lephant plodding through the rainforest
S loths sleep all day
T oucans go *squawk.*

Sophie Pearce-Molland (6)
The Grey House School, Hartley Wintney

The Rainforest

R ain pouring in-between the plants, the plants rustling in the wind
A nimals chasing each other every day
I nsects crawling in the leaves
N oisy animals screeching very loud
F lowers shooting every day
O rang-utan swinging from tree to tree
R ivers splashing along the rocks
E lephants trumping along
S winging monkey
T rees sway.

Isobel Young (6)
The Grey House School, Hartley Wintney

My First Acrostic - Southern Counties

The Rainforest

R attlesnake slithering
A rmy ants marching
I nsects hurdling
N oises everywhere
F at big elephants
O rang-utans swinging
R iver flowing
E lephants running
S loth asleep
T oucan squawking.

Charlie Warren (6)
The Grey House School, Hartley Wintney

The Rainforest

R attlesnakes rattling
A nts stealing
I tching monkeys
N oise everywhere
F lowers grow
O rang-utans banging
R iver floating
E lephants sucking water
S nakes sliding
T igers leaping.

Louis Sykes (5)
The Grey House School, Hartley Wintney

My First Acrostic - Southern Counties

The Rainforest

R ain comes in the rainforest
A toucan on a tree
I nsects crawling
N oise is loud
F rogs ribbiting
O rang-utan
R attlesnakes
E xcited frogs
S treams going fast
T oucans jumping.

Alfie Smallwood (6)
The Grey House School, Hartley Wintney

The Rainforest

R aining in the rainforest on the green leaves
A nts are on the rainforest's wet floor
I nsects buzzing around me
N oise of snakes hissing
F lowers growing fast
O rang-utans swinging from tree to tree
R attlesnakes rattling
E lephants walking along
S loth sleeping all day
T oucans being very naughty.

Finlay Anderson (6)
The Grey House School, Hartley Wintney

My First Acrostic - Southern Counties

The Rainforest

R attlesnakes go through the leaves and go up the trees
A rmy ants crawl on the ground
I nsects are lovely
N ectar is beautiful
F lowers are pretty
O rang-utans are furry and cuddly
R abbits are cute
E lephants have trunks
S loths move slowly up the trees
T igers are scary.

Luca Tonkin (6)
The Grey House School, Hartley Wintney

The Rainforest

R attlesnakes rattling in the grass
A rmy ants marching in the rainforest
I nsects crawling on the leaves
N ectar blowing in the breeze
F loating flowers in the breeze
O rang-utans jumping up and down on the branch
R abbit is going into the burrow, going to feed its babies
E lephant is stamping in the jungle
S loths slowly move in the trees
T he toucan is squawking in the tree.

Amelia Trist (6)
The Grey House School, Hartley Wintney

My First Acrostic - Southern Counties

The Rainforest

R ain in the rainforest and lots of animals
A nts that bite
I mpossible flowers in the rainforest
N oisy animals
F antastic colours
O rang-utan swinging in the trees
R iver that makes a lot of noise
E lephants suck the water in the lakes
S nakes hissing
T igers sneaking through the grass.

Frida Kenning (5)
The Grey House School, Hartley Wintney

Young Writers Information

We hope you have enjoyed reading this book - and that you will continue to enjoy it in the coming years.

If you like reading and writing poetry drop us a line, or give us a call, and we'll send you a free information pack.

Alternatively if you would like to order further copies of this book or any of our other titles, then please give us a call or log onto our website at www.youngwriters.co.uk.

Young Writers Information
Remus House
Coltsfoot Drive
Peterborough
PE2 9JX
(01733) 890066